FROM THE LIBRARY OF

Forget Me Notes
From Niederbipp with Love

Copyright © 2011 by Benjamin A. Behunin
All rights reserved. Manufactured in the United States of America

First printing, November 2011

Published by

Abendmahl Press
P.O. Box 581083
Salt Lake City, Utah 84158-1083

ISBN: 978-0-9838025-1-8

Artwork by Ben Behunin and of historical origins
Designed by Ben Behunin and Bert Compton
Layout by Bert Compton- Compton Design Studio
All scriptural references are from the King James
Translation of the Bible.

Forget Me Notes

From Niederbipp with Love

by Benjamin A. Behunin

DEDICATED TO ALL THOSE WHO BELIEVE IN NIEDERBIPP.

Prelude

Have you ever gone looking for something, only to discover it's been right under your nose the whole time? I know I have–probably thousands of times. And then there are the millions of other things that I've missed along my journey simply because I'm too busy to notice, or am somehow otherwise oblivious.

Over the past couple of years, I have been asked countless times about the Forget-me-nots that weave their way throughout each of the Isaac books. Where do they come from? What do they mean? Why did you include them in Isaac's special tea? My answer is always the same. I did not put them in the tea. I did not make up the story. I wish I had, but the meaning and the stories came to me in what I can only explain as a bolt of pure inspiration. As to their meaning—well, I can only tell you what I know.

It seems the best things in life are often found in the smallest of packages. Many of us have Forget-me-nots growing in our gardens in the early spring. They often grow spontaneously, right under our noses, without us even taking notice. And why should we? They are, after all, one of the smallest flowers in the garden. I have learned in recent years that, like the forget-me-nots in my garden, God's love also springs up spontaneously, right under our noses, and can easily be missed if we're not looking for it. For me, through the writing of The Niederbipp Trilogy, or the "Isaac books" as they are commonly called, the Forget-Me-Not flower has come to symbolize the love that God has for all of his children—you, and me, and all of us.

When you print your own books, you get to name your own press. I chose Abendmahl Press. Abendmahl is a German word. Literally translated, it means evening meal. If you look at the logo at either the front or the back of my books, you will see the images of wheat and grapes. A Google search reveals that this is more than just the symbols of a harvest. Look it up and you will find images of Leonardo da Vinci's *The Last Supper*. It was here that Christ introduced his chosen apostles to one of the most meaningful symbols known in Christendom—the bread and the wine of His sacrament.

If you have read The Niederbipp Trilogy at face value, I hope you have enjoyed a good, moral story of a just and humble potter who changed the lives of everyone he met. But, if you have read the books, looking for symbols, you have likely discovered something infinitely deeper and more powerful. If you choose to read them again, may I suggest one question that may lead to a deeper understanding. Beyond his wisdom and love, what was it that Isaac shared with everyone who came to his shop? If your answer is that he broke bread with them, and shared with them a very special drink that helped them to remember the love of God, then you are on the right track to discovering who Isaac really was.

In the following pages, I hope you will discover—or rediscover, as I have, some of the gems of The Niederbipp Trilogy. There are beautiful nuggets of truth from people as diverse as Buddha and Jimi Hendrix, but the wisdom, truth and insight they offer have hopefully inspired us all.

The words in this book have all been gleaned from the pages of The Niederbipp Trilogy. There is nothing new. And yet as I have read these words again in a new and different context, they seem to stand a little taller and reach a little deeper into my heart and mind. I suppose that's the way truth works—the more we hear it, the truer it becomes.

And so my friends, with that, I give you *Forget-Me-Notes: From Niederbipp, With Love*. As you read these things again, let it be as if for the first time. And may you never forget the love God has for you.

Your friend—

Ben

Christmas 2011

SILENTLY, ONE BY ONE, IN THE
INFINITE MEADOWS OF HEAVEN,
BLOSSOMED THE LOVELY STARS,
THE FORGET-ME-NOTS OF THE ANGELS.
—HENRY WADSWORTH LONGFELLOW,
IN EVANGELINE

The forget-me-not is a subtle reminder to us that all that we have comes from God and that it is meant to be shared.

Tom in Becoming Isaac, pg. 311

The Only Gift is a Portion of Thyself.

– Ralph Waldo Emerson –

GOD ENTERS BY A PRIVATE DOOR
INTO EVERY INDIVIDUAL.
- RALPH WALDO EMERSON -

We make a living by what we get, but we make a life by what we give.

— Winston Churchill —

Gather Ye Rosebuds While Ye May...
—Robert Herrick—

THOUGH WE TRAVEL THE WORLD OVER TO FIND THE BEAUTIFUL, WE MUST CARRY IT WITH US OR WE FIND IT NOT. ~RALPH WALDO EMERSON~

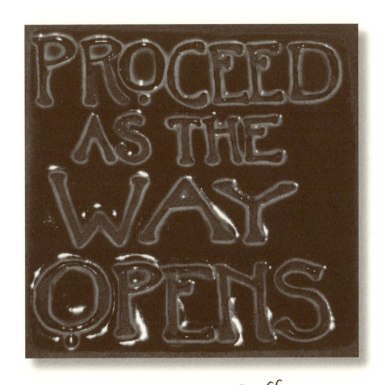

Follow your bliss and the universe will open doors for you where there were only walls.

— Joseph Campbell —

True love does not come by finding a perfect person, but by learning to see an imperfect person perfectly.

— Jason Jordan —

DO NOT EXPECT MORE LIGHT UNTIL YOU FOLLOW WHAT YOU HAVE.

— QUAKER PROVERB —

THE BEST ANSWERS IN LIFE ARE THE ONES THE UNIVERSE WHISPERS IN OUR EARS AFTER WE'VE ASKED THE RIGHT QUESTIONS AND MADE OUR INVESTMENT.

ERIC - BECOMING ISAAC - PG 202

Perhaps our own reiterated cries deafen us to the voice we hope to hear.

– C.S. Lewis –

... the world has many different names for God, but I've found in my travels that with love and understanding, there is always more that makes men brothers than anything that makes them foes. Focusing on differences erects walls between neighbors—walls that dam us and our progression as members of the human family.

Eric in Becoming Isaac, pg. 198

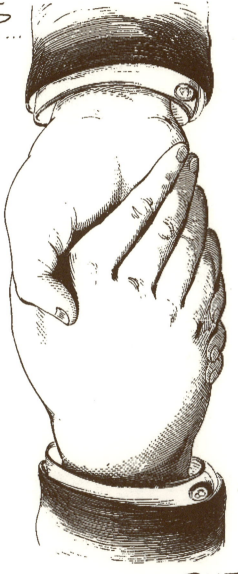

IT IS NOT ENOUGH TO HELP THE FEEBLE UP...

BUT TO SUPPORT HIM AFTER

-SHAKESPEARE-

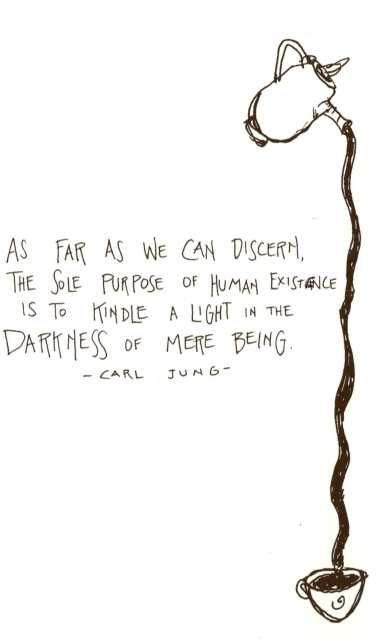

As far as we can discern, the sole purpose of human existence is to kindle a light in the darkness of mere being.
— Carl Jung —

WHEN THE POWER OF LOVE
OVERCOMES THE LOVE OF POWER,
THE WORLD WILL KNOW PEACE
—JIMI HENDRIX—

IT IS THE EYE OF OTHER PEOPLE THAT RUIN US.

IF I WERE BLIND I WOULD WANT NEITHER FINE CLOTHES, FINE HOUSES OR FINE FURNITURE.
— BENJAMIN FRANKLIN —

You cannot learn love from a book or a lecture, only by conquering our selfishness can we know the pure love of God.

Thomas in Remembering Isaac, pg. 334

A SINGLE DAY
IS ENOUGH
TO MAKE US
A LITTLE LARGER.

-PAUL KLEE-

"We shall not cease from exploration, and the end of all our exploring will be to arrive where we started and know the place for the first time." —T.S. Eliot

Cheers to the Journey

THE SPIRIT OF MAN IS THE CANDLE OF THE LORD.
PROVERBS 20:27

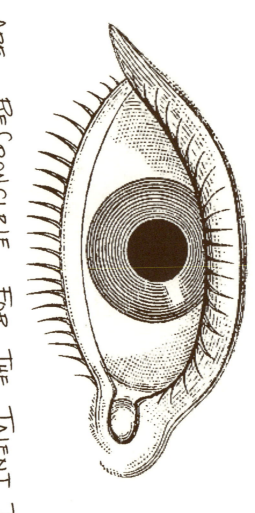

WORK WHILE YOU HAVE THE LIGHT.

YOU ARE RESPONSIBLE FOR THE TALENT THAT HAS BEEN ENTRUSTED TO YOU.

- HENRI-FREDRIC AMIEL -

TRUE GODLINESS DOESN'T TURN MEN OUT OF THE WORLD, BUT ENABLES THEM TO LIVE BETTER IN IT, AND EXCITES THEIR ENDEAVORS TO MEND IT.

—WILLIAM PENN—

Infancy is the perpetual Messiah, which comes into the arms of fallen men, and pleads with them to return to paradise.
— Ralph Waldo Emerson —

THE DOORSTEP TO THE TEMPLE OF WISDOM IS A KNOWLEDGE OF OUR OWN IGNORANCE.

—BENJAMIN FRANKLIN—

IF THOU WOULDST BE HAPPY...

HAVE AN INDIFFERENCE FOR MORE THAN WHAT IS SUFFICIENT.

—WILLIAM PENN—

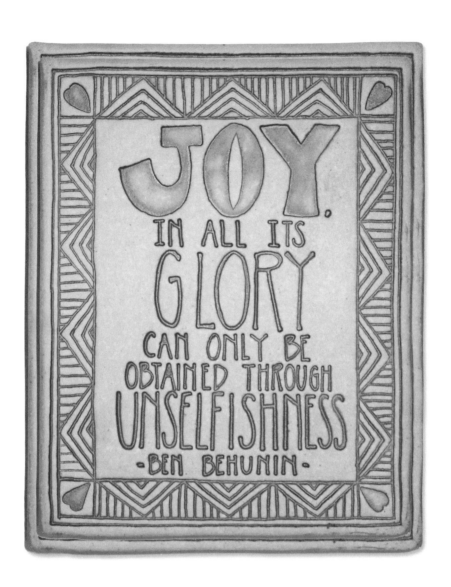

Too often we underestimate the power of a touch, a smile, a kind word, a listening ear, an honest compliment, or the smallest act of caring, all of which have the potential to turn a life around.
— Leo Buscaglia —

Darkness cannot drive out darkness., only light can do that. Hate cannot drive out hate, only love can do that.

Martin Luther King Jr.

IF YOU LOOK FOR TRUTH, YOU MAY FIND
COMFORT IN THE END;
IF YOU LOOK FOR COMFORT, YOU WILL NOT GET
EITHER COMFORT OR TRUTH, ONLY SOFT SOAP
AND WISHFUL THINKING TO BEGIN,
AND IN THE END, DESPAIR.
—C. S. LEWIS—

"WHEN YOU PRAY, MOVE YOUR FEET."

-QUAKER PROVERB-

> THERE IS BUT ONE
> CAUSE OF MAN'S
> FAILURE
> AND THAT IS
> MAN'S LACK OF
> FAITH
> IN HIS TRUE
> SELF.
> —WILLIAM JAMES—

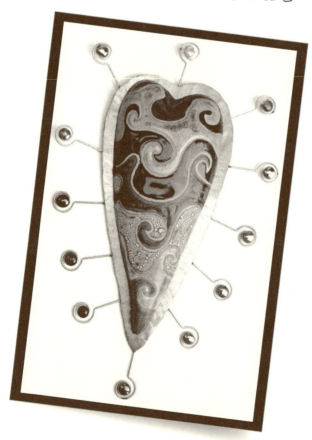

When you examine the lives of the most influential people who have ever walked among us, you discover one thread that winds through them all. They have been aligned first with their spiritul nature and only then with their physical selves.
—Albert Einstein—

... when one seeks truth, he always goes away with more than he asks for.

Thomas in Discovering Isaac, pg.. 334.

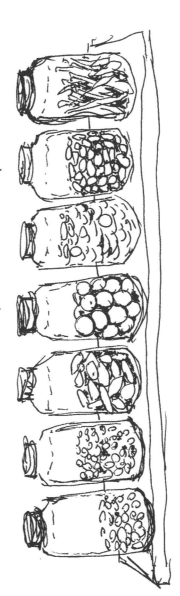

God cannot give us a happiness and peace apart from Himself because it is not there—

There is no such thing.

— C.S. Lewis —

THE HIGHEST REVELATION IS THAT GOD IS IN EVERY MAN.
— RALPH WALDO EMERSON —

The more I observe people, the more I realize most of us are broken souls who are blinded by our own brokenness.

Jake in Becoming Isaac, pg. 122

Let us take the risks of PEACE upon our lives, not impose the risks of WAR upon the world.

— Quaker Proverb —

Love is a portion of the soul itself, and it is of the same nature as the celestial atmosphere of paradise —

Victor Hugo

I EXPECT TO PASS
THROUGH THIS LIFE
BUT ONCE. IF THEREFORE,
THERE BE ANY KINDNESS
I CAN SHOW, OR ANY GOOD
THING I CAN DO TO ANY
FELLOW BEING, LET ME DO
IT NOW, AND NOT DEFER OR
NEGLECT IT, AS I SHALL
NOT PASS THIS WAY AGAIN.

—WILLIAM PENN—

... there is a big difference between covering a sliver with a Band-Aid and taking the sliver out. I have learned that for most slivers, we are incapable of removing them ourselves. I have witnessed the change that comes into people's lives when they learn that only the hands which have been pierced with nails are sensitive enough to remove the slivers from our hands ... and souls and apply the healing balm we all need.

Charlie in Becoming Isaac, pg. 93

Anything you cannot relinquish when it has outlived its usefulness, possesses you, and in this materialistic age, a great many of us are possessed by our possessions.
— Peace Pilgrim —

One may not reach the dawn save by the path of night.

—Kahlil Gibran—

ART IS THE HEALING
OINTMENT OOZES FROM
OUR HEARTS AND MINDS AND
HEALS OUR ACHING WORLD.

— FRED BABB —

We can't fight fear with fear. We can't scare people into sobriety. We can't force them to walk the line. The only answer is love.

Charlie in Remembering Isaac, pg. 121

... love is free. The only currency exchanged in the transaction of love is love. Everything else is a counterfeit.

Jodi in Remembering Isaac, pg. 121

KEEP AWAY FROM THOSE WHO TRY TO BELITTLE YOUR AMBITIONS. SMALL PEOPLE ALWAYS DO THAT, BUT THE REALLY GREAT MAKE YOU BELIEVE THAT YOU, TOO, CAN BECOME GREAT.
—MARK TWAIN—

HE WHO WANTS TO DO GOOD
KNOCKS AT THE GATE;
HE WHO LOVES FINDS THE DOOR OPEN.
—RABINDRANATH TAGORE—

Following the path of truth will never exempt us from trial and heartache, but it does give purpose and understanding to our hardships if we allow ourselves to be taught and if we seek for answers.

Eric in Becoming Isaac, pg. 188

But the path of the just is as the shining light, that shineth more and more unto the perfect day.

Proverbs 4:18

When all that you retain is loveable there is no reason for fear to remain with you.

— A Course in Miracles —

The darkness of this world knows the power of light. It does all it can to try to snuff it out—to discourage us from developing the talents with which we've been entrusted. It aims to keep us from nurturing that light before it has the power to shatter the darkness.

Eric in Becoming Isaac, pg. 200

FORGIVENESS DOES NOT CHANGE THE PAST, BUT IT DOES ENLARGE THE FUTURE.

—PAUL BOESE—

"Life is thickly sown with thorns, and I know no other remedy than to pass quickly through them. The longer we dwell on our misfortunes, the greater is their power to harm us."
—Voltaire—

Stay Hungry
—Plato—

We live, in fact, in a world starved for solitude, silence and private: and therefore starved for meditation & true friendship.
— C. S. Lewis —

Just as a candle cannot burn without fire,
men cannot live without a spiritual life.
—Buddah

Money has never made man happy, nor will it; there is nothing in its nature to produce happiness. The more of it one has, the more one wants.
— Benjamin Franklin —

... there is no room
for greed or envy
when you live your
life based on love
instead of fear.

Tom in Becoming
Isaac, pg. 312

"There are only two mistakes one can make along the road to truth; not going all the way, and not starting." – Buddha

Life is really simple, but we insist on making it complicated.
— Confucius —

Simplicity Rocks

As you simplify your life, the laws of the universe will be simpler; solitude will not be solitude, poverty will will not be poverty, nor weakness-weakness.
— Henry David Thoreau —

MONEY IS NOT REQUIRED TO BUY ONE NECESSITY OF THE SOUL.
— HENRY DAVID THOREAU —

Love is the simplest of all of God's gifts, but it can only remain simple if we forgive–if we can turn our weapons of war into building blocks.

Emma in Becoming Isaac, pg. 309

IF YOU WILL MAKE LISTENING AND OBSERVATION YOUR OCCUPATION YOU WILL GAIN MUCH MORE THAN YOU CAN BY TALK.
— ROBERT BADEN-POWELL —

> He, who blinded by ambition, raises himself to a position whence he cannot mount higher, must thereafter fall with the greatest loss.
>
> — Niccolo Machiavelli —

THERE IS NO REVENGE SO COMPLETE AS FORGIVESS.

—JOSH BILLINGS—

Let your love be like the misty rain, coming softly, but flooding the river.

— Madagascan Proverb —

You cannot teach a man anything, you can only help him find it within himself.
– Galileo Galilei –

Tradition is a two-edged resource. It can give us a foundation to build upon, but if left unexamined and unquestioned, those same traditions can bind us down and halt our progression.

Thomas in Discovering Isaac, pg. 331

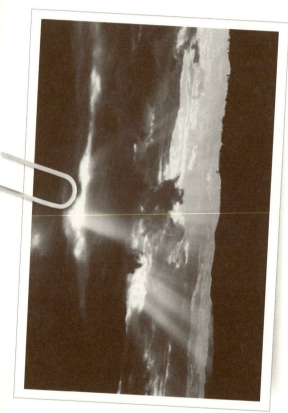

Every man must decide whether he will walk in the light of creative altruism or in the darkness of destructive selfishness.
— Martin Luther King Jr. —

> To better hear the world outside, listen faithfully to the voice inside.
> — Quaker Proverb —

WE MUST BE **LOVERS**, AND AT ONCE THE IMPOSSIBLE BECOMES **POSSIBLE**.
— RALPH WALDO EMERSON —

Trust is a fragile thing, but it can be rebuilt, one stone at a time.

Emma in Becoming Isaac, pg. 305

IT IS BY SUFFERING THAT HUMAN BEINGS BECOME ANGELS

— VICTOR HUGO —

Rocks are the baggage we carry when we are unable or unwilling to forgive. Instead of forgiving and letting the sorrow go, we allow it to fester and grow until it becomes hard and heavy and sometimes jagged.

Emma in Becoming Isaac, pg. 308

IT IS IN THE PARDONING THAT WE ARE PARDONED

— St Francis of Assisi —

God's light, with its full spectrum of color, enters every human heart, customized to the person who receives it.

Eric in Becoming Isaac, pg. 201

The wise man in the storm prays to God, not for safety from danger, but for deliverance from fear.
—Ralph Waldo Emerson—

The act of being still, of meditating and pondering is something that has largely been lost in our world of 24-7 news coverage and our perceived need for constant entertainment. Is it any wonder that the things of God have been washed away by this flood of noise and chaos?

Thomas in Discovering Isaac, pg. 332

CONTENT MAKES POOR MEN RICH. DISCONTENT MAKES RICH MEN POOR

— BENJAMIN FRANKLIN —

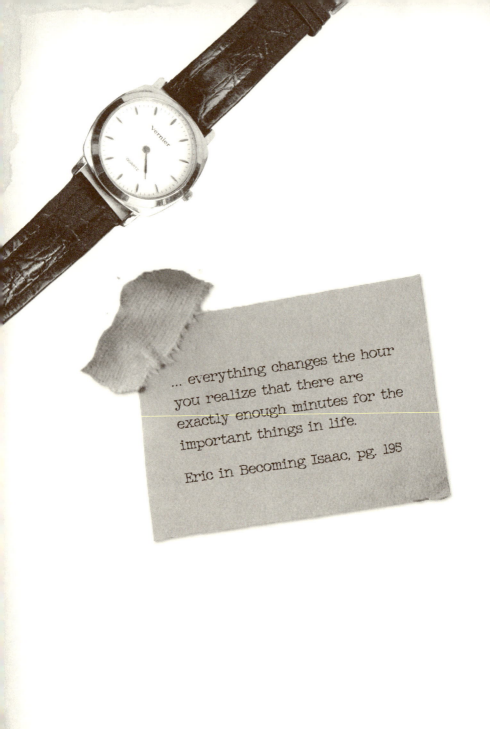

... everything changes the hour you realize that there are exactly enough minutes for the important things in life.

Eric in Becoming Isaac, pg. 195

THE MAN WHO REMOVES A MOUNTAIN BEGINS BY CARRYING AWAY SMALL STONES.
—WILLIAM FAULKNER

... changing the world begins with a change of heart.

Eric in Becoming Isaac, pg. 197

The only devils in this world are those running around in our own hearts, and that is where our battles should be fought.

—Mahatma Gandhi—

It's a sad thing to try and fail, but it's even sadder to fail because you never tried.

Jake in Remembering Isaac, pg. 260

Don't be discouraged by failure. It can be a positive experience. Failure is, in a sense, the highway to success, inasmuch as every discovery of what is false leads us to seek earnestly after what is true, and every fresh experience points out some form of error which we shall afterwards carefully avoid. — John Keats

Each day is a new day with its own challenges and heartache, but every day also brings with it the opportunity for learning and greatness.

Eric in Becoming Isaac, pg. 188

Mutual respect, when coupled with faith, endowed with grace, and unselfishly nurtured, has the unique ability to make love blossom and grow exponentially more powerful.

- Ben Behunin -

IF YOU BREAK YOUR NECK,
IF YOU HAVE NOTHING TO EAT,
IF YOUR HOUSE IS ON FIRE,
  THEN YOU GOT A PROBLEM.
EVERYTHING ELSE IS INCONVENIENCE
      — ROBERT FULGHUM —

WORK AND STRUGGLE AND NEVER ACCEPT AN EVIL THAT YOU CAN CHANGE

— ANDRE GIDE —

The Garden of Eden was just a nice place to live before Adam and Eve were cast out of it. Then it became paradise. We rarely appreciate how good things are until they change. Take it from a florist, the reality of life is this: We have to bloom where we are planted, enjoy the sunlight while we can, and thank the heavens for the rain that not only beats us down, but feeds us and makes us stronger.

Gloria in Remembering Isaac, pg. 214

THE TRUTH THAT
MAKES MEN
FREE
IS FOR THE MOST
PART THE TRUTH
WHICH MEN PREFER
NOT TO HEAR.
— HERBERT AGAR —

"Hope is a thing with feathers that perches in the soul and sings a tune without words and never stops at all." — Emily Dickinson

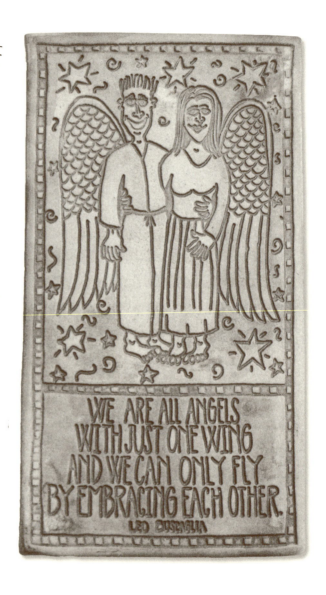

He that cannot forgive others,
breaks the bridge over which
he himself must pass if he
would ever reach heaven,
for everyone has need
to be forgiven.
- George Herbert -

I don't know if we can fully appreciate the need for forgiveness until we recognize our own brokenness.

Emma in Becoming Isaac, pg. 305

THERE IS NO SITUATION THAT IS NOT TRANSFORMABLE.
THERE IS NO PERSON WHO IS HOPELESS.
THERE IS NO SET OF CIRCUMSTANCES
THAT CANNOT BE TURNED ABOUT BY
ORDINARY HUMAN BEINGS
AND THEIR NATURAL CAPACITY
FOR LOVE OF THE DEEPEST SORT.
— ARCHBISHOP DESMOND TUTU —

First, learn from the past that you may be a better husband, a better father, a better potter and a better man than the generations before you. And second, carve your path straight and wide for those that follow.

Isaac in Discovering Isaac, pg. 341

AND EVERY ONE THAT LOVETH IS BORN OF GOD AND KNOWETH GOD...FOR GOD IS LOVE.

1 JOHN 4:7

BELOVED, LET US LOVE ONE ANOTHER: FOR LOVE IS OF GOD;

MANY OF LIFE'S FAILURES ARE PEOPLE WHO DID NOT REALIZE HOW CLOSE THEY WERE TO SUCCESS WHEN THEY GAVE UP —THOMAS EDISON—

We are unlimited beings. We have no ceiling. The capabilities and the talents and the gifts and the power that is within every single individual that is on this planet, is unlimited.
—Michael Beckwith—

We all have light to share with each other; we all have something to give. If each of us has a seed of godliness within us, then there must be within each of us a portion of greatness.

Eric in Becoming Isaac, pg. 201

> Our duty, as men and women, is to proceed as if limits to our ability do not exist. We are collaborators in creation.
>
> — Pierre Teilhard de Chardin —

There is a world of difference between truth and facts. Facts can obscure the truth.
— Maya Angelou —

The way of peace is the way of love
— Peace Pilgrim —

For light,
I go directly
to the source
of light,
not to any
of the
reflections.

— Peace Pilgrim —

Most of us require a heavy dose of humility before we wake up to the truths that are all around us, waiting anxiously to speak to us. ... the truth is nearly always easier to live than its alternative. It's us and our clouded, uninspired vision that makes our lives difficult, leading us to wander blindly down crooked paths and lose our way.

Thomas in Discovering Isaac, pg. 333

FORGIVENESS IS THE FRAGRANCE THE VIOLET SHEDS ON THE HEEL THAT HAS CRUSHED IT.
- MARK TWAIN -

THE MOST IMPORTANT PART OF PRAYER IS WHAT WE FEEL, NOT WHAT WE SAY.

WE SPEND A GREAT DEAL OF TIME TELLING GOD WHAT WE THINK SHOULD BE DONE AND NOT ENOUGH TIME WAITING IN THE STILLNESS FOR GOD TO TELL US WHAT TO DO.

—PEACE PILGRIM—

All I have teaches me to trust the Creator for all I have not seen.

—Ralph Waldo Emerson—

Two roads diverged in a wood, and I — I took the one less traveled by, and that has made all the difference — Robert Frost

It seems we often don't appeal to Him until we're in crisis mode. Part of that is because of our lack of humility. We feel like we can take the reins for a while when the trail is smooth. The problem is, when the trail is smooth for too long, we fall asleep and forget the horse and buggy belong to someone else. We usually don't ask for instructions or directions until the horse is hanging over a hundred foot cliff and the buggy is dangling on the edge. I think the response we get at those times is often very different than if we'd remained alert during the whole journey and asked for directions every mile or so. Humility seems to be the key to our answers and the timing in which they're received.

Susan in Discovering Isaac, pg.. 266.

But now, oh Lord, thou art our Father, we are the clay, and thou our Potter, and we are all the work of thy hands.

Isaiah 64:8

There is no greater agony than bearing an untold story inside you.

—Maya Angelou—

ARISE, AND GO DOWN TO THE POTTER'S HOUSE, AND THERE I WILL CAUSE THEE TO HEAR MY WORDS.

JEREMIAH 18:2

Ben enjoys hearing from his readers. You can reach him at:

Abendmahl Press
P.O. Box 581083
Salt Lake City, Utah 84158-1083

Or by email to
benbehunin@comcast.net

More information on this book is available at
www.amazon.com
www.rememberingisaac.blogspot.com
And www.vivaniederbipp.com
and on Facebook
Ben's pottery is available at www.potterboy.com
and many fine galleries across the U.S.A.

If you would like to feature the Niederbipp Trilogy
in your book club, please contact Ben for a group discount.

For speaking engagements including book clubs and inaugurations
please call (801) 883-0146

For design information, contact Bert Compton at bert@comptonds.com